P9-DNO-053

VOL. 3
Action Edition

Story and Art by
RUMIKO TAKAHASHI

English Adaptation/Gerard Jones
Translation/Mari Morimoto
Touch-Up Art & Lettering/Wayne Truman
Cover Design/Hidemi Sahara
Graphics & Design/Sean Lee
Editor (1st Edition)/Julie Davis
Editor (Action Edition)/Julie Davis

Managing Editor/Annette Roman
Editor in Chief/William Flanagan
Dir. of Licensing and Acquisitions/Rika Inouye
Sr. VP of Sales & Marketing/Rick Bauer
Sr. VP of Editorial/Hyoe Narita
Publisher/Seiji Horibuchi

INUYASHA is rated "T+" for Older Teens. It may contain violence, language, alcohol or tobacco use, or suggestive situations.

© 1997 Rumiko Takahashi/Shogakukan, Inc. First published by Shogakukan, Inc. in Japan as "Inuyasha."

INUYASHA is a trademark of VIZ, LLC. © 2003 VIZ, LLC. All rights reserved. No unauthorized reproduction allowed.

New and adapted artwork and text
© 2003 VIZ, LLC

All rights reserved.

The stories, characters and incidents mentioned in this publication are entirely fictional. For the purposes of publication in English, the artwork in this publication is printed in reverse from the original Japanese version.

Printed in Canada.

Published by VIZ, LLC
P.O. Box 77010
San Francisco, CA 94107

1st Edition published 1998

Action Edition
10 9 8 7 6 5 4 3 2 1
First printing, June 2003

www.viz.com

store.viz.com

INUYASHA

VOL. 3

Action Edition

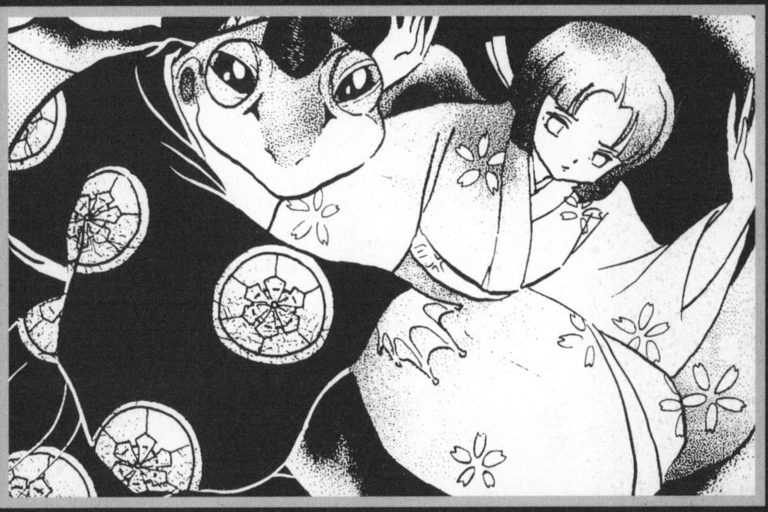

STORY AND ART BY

RUMIKO TAKAHASHI

CONTENTS

THE STORY THUS FAR

Long ago, in the "Warring States" era of Japan's Muromachi period (Sengoku-jidai, approximately 1467-1568 CE), a legendary doglike half-demon called "Inu-Yasha" attempted to steal the Shikon Jewel, or "Jewel of Four Souls," from a village, but was stopped by the enchanted arrow of the village priestess, Kikyo. Inu-Yasha fell into a deep sleep, pinned to a tree by Kikyo's arrow, while the mortally wounded Kikyo took the Shikon Jewel with her into the fires of her funeral pyre. Years passed.

Fast forward to the present day. Kagome, a Japanese high school girl, is pulled into a well one day by a mysterious centipede monster, and finds herself transported into the past, only to come face to face with the trapped Inu-Yasha. She frees him, and Inu-Yasha easily defeats the centipede monster.

The residents of the village, now fifty years older, readily accept Kagome as the reincarnation of their deceased priestess Kikyo, a claim supported by the fact that the Shikon Jewel emerges from a cut on Kagome's body. Unfortunately, the jewel's rediscovery means that the village is soon under attack by a variety of demons in search of this treasure. Then, the jewel is accidentally shattered into many shards, each of which may have the fearsome power of the entire jewel.

Although Inu-Yasha says he hates Kagome because of her resemblance to Kikyo, the woman who "killed" him, he is forced to team up with her when Kaede, the village leader, binds him to Kagome with a powerful spell. Now the two grudging companions must fight to reclaim and reassemble the shattered shards of the Shikon Jewel before they fall into the wrong hands.

THIS VOLUME A young retainer, an immortal frog, a battle to rescue a princess, and a horror handed down through the ages.

INU-YASHA
A half-human, half-demon hybrid, Inu-Yasha has doglike ears, a thick mane of white hair, and demonic strength. Hoping to increase his demonic powers, he once stole the Shikon Jewel from a village, but was cast into a fifty-year sleep by the arrow of the village priestess, Kikyo, who died as a result of the battle. Now, he assists Kagome in her search for the shards of the Jewel, mostly because he has no choice in the matter—a charmed necklace allows Kagome to restrain him with a single word.

KIKYO
A village priestess who was the original protector of the Shikon Jewel. She died fifty years ago.

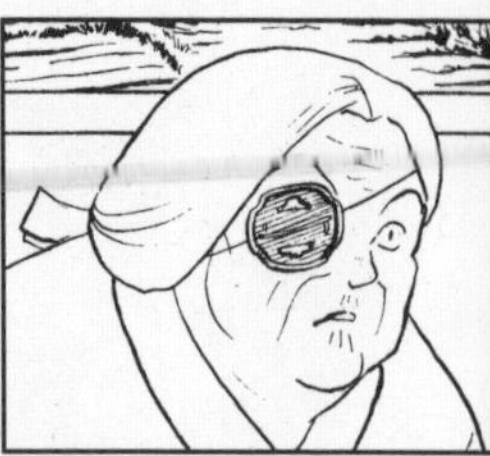

KAEDE
Kikyo's little sister, now an old woman and the leader of the village. She cast the spell on the necklace that allows Kagome to control Inu-Yasha.

KAGOME
A Japanese schoolgirl from the modern day who is also the reincarnation of Kikyo, the priestess who imprisoned Inu-Yasha for fifty years with her enchanted arrow. As Kikyo's reincarnation, Kagome has the power to see the Shikon Jewel shards, even ones hidden within a demon's body.

SCROLL ONE

THE DARK CASTLE

YES! SHARDS OF THE JEWEL OF FOUR SOULS!
DO YOU *KNOW* OF IT?!
JEWEL OF FOUR SOULS?
YOU MEAN THE ONE THAT INCREASES YOUR MAGIC POWERS IF YOU POSSESS IT?
THEN YOU *DO* KNOW IT!
HE'S ASKING IF WE KNOW IT?
KNOW WHAT?

THREE DAYS, INU-YASHA...
THREE DAYS SINCE WE LEFT THE VILLAGE...
AND WE HAVEN'T YET FOUND A CLUE!
BWA
I KNOW, I KNOW.
MAYBE THE SHARDS JUST AREN'T IN MUSASHI'S DOMAIN.
EH?
SCHH...
OHHH, THAT FEELS GOOD!

SHFF...

HM?

EEEEEEE!!

YAA!!!

fweeeee
AAH, YOU'RE A GOOD LAD, HIYASHIMARU.
THIS IS NOT *FOOD*...!
WHAT...?
SHH

YOU MUST BE THIEVES!
IDENTIFY YOUR-SELVES!
VSH
GIVE ME BACK MY CLOTHES!
HO, THERE!
HSH

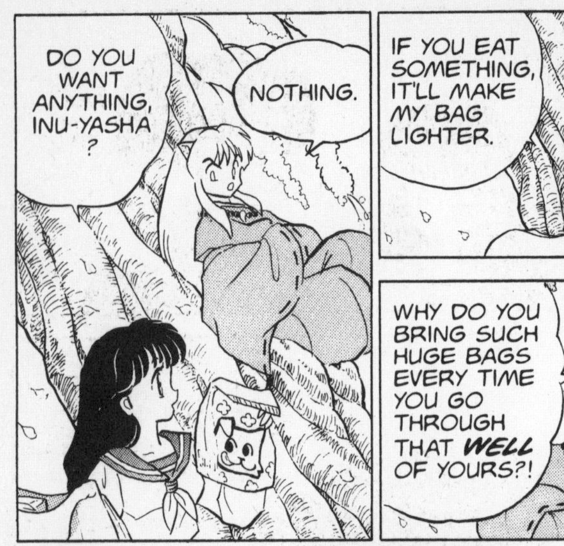
DO YOU WANT ANYTHING, INU-YASHA?
NOTHING.

IF YOU EAT SOMETHING, IT'LL MAKE MY BAG LIGHTER.
WILL IT NOW...?
WHY DO YOU BRING SUCH HUGE BAGS EVERY TIME YOU GO THROUGH THAT *WELL* OF YOURS?!
I HAVE TO CHANGE MY CLOTHES... GET MY HOMEWORK...

THESE DRIED TUBERS WERE A BLESSING
BAM
EXTRA SALT
A THOUSAND THANKS, MY LADY.

UM...
MY NAME'S KAGOME.
AND THIS IS INU-YASHA.
AND THIS...
SLURRRRP
MNG MNG MNG
WHAP
GOOSH
IS MYŌGA... THE FLEA.
WHAT *ARE* THESE CREATURES?
FLICK

BUT I AM CALLED NOBUNAGA.

NOBUNAGA--?!

I'M SORRY, BUT...

...I AM NOT OF THE ODA CLAN.

HUH...?

YOU'RE NOT?!

TIME IS SLIPPING AWAY.

I MUST BE GOING.

RMM

I AM OF THE TAKEDA CLAN.

AND I AM *NOT* PLEASED TO BE TAKEN FOR THAT "SUPREME IDIOT."

D'YE SEE NOW? YE CAN'T HIDE 'EM FROM *US*!

WHAT TH'LORD WANTS... TH'LORD'LL SURELY *HAVE*!

KLOP KLOP...

NO... NO...

THEN IT MUST BE TRUE...

THE LORD OF THIS DOMAIN MUST SURELY...
...HAVE GONE MAD !!

DO YOU REALLY THINK WE COULD LET HIM GO OFF ON HIS *OWN*?!
HEY.
WHY DO WE HAVE TO FOLLOW THIS IDIOT AROUND?

'THOUGH THE GODS MAY STRIKE ME DOWN FOR SPEAKIN' IT...

...'TIS SAID OUR LORD IS POSSESSED BY A DEMON!
POING!
MOOSH...

zeehh... zeehh...

HUHH.

HUHH. HUHH.

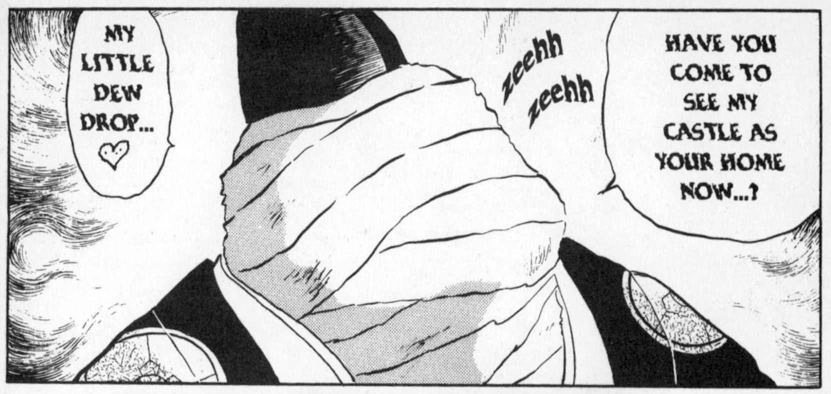
HAVE YOU COME TO SEE MY CASTLE AS YOUR HOME NOW...?
zeehh zeehh
MY LITTLE DEW DROP... ♡

I MUST NOT LET HIM HEAR MY FEAR...
M-MY LORD, I...
I LACK FOR NOTHING HERE...

MY... MY LORD?
YES... ♡?

...THE GROWTH OF HIS GIRTH...THE STRANGENESS IN HIS VOICE...
...REPEL ME AS MUCH AS HE ONCE ATTRACTED ME.

I MUST NOT LET HIM SENSE THAT THE CHANGES THIS DISEASE HAVE WROUGHT IN HIM...
HUHH... HUHH...
A SWEET SOUND... TO MY EARS...

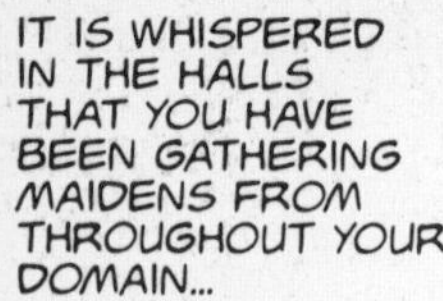
IT IS WHISPERED IN THE HALLS THAT YOU HAVE BEEN GATHERING MAIDENS FROM THROUGHOUT YOUR DOMAIN...

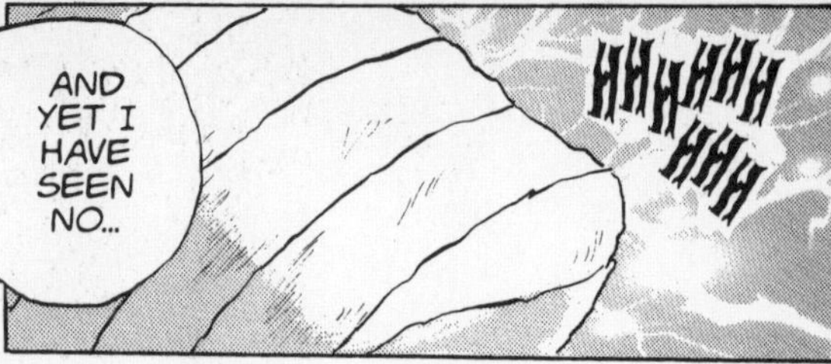
AND YET I HAVE SEEN NO...
HHHHHHHHH

gasp
BAMM
IT IS NOT FOR YOU TO KNOW !!

Y-YOUR FORGIVENESS, MY LORD!
I...I SPOKE OUT OF PLACE.

PLEASE, SOMEONE... ANYONE...

PLEASE HELP ME...
PLEASE TAKE ME HOME!

IT'S NOT JUST A RUMOR...

THE SMELL OF DEMON IS THICK IN THE AIR.
AND WHERE THERE'S A DEMON... THERE MAY BE A JEWEL!

WE'RE GOING TO SCALE IT IN ONE LEAP.
HANG ON TIGHT, KAGOME.
O-KAY!

I, TOO, HAVE BUSINESS IN THIS CASTLE!
HEY, WHO INVITED *YOU*?!

TPP

BE BRAVE... JUST A LITTLE LONGER...
PRINCESS TSUYU...

SHA
LET'S GO!

WHAT DO YOU MEAN, OLD BUG?
WATCH WHERE YOU HOP!
INU-YASHA... THERE'S SOMETHING WRONG HERE.

A CASTLE OF THIS SIZE...
...AND NOT A SINGLE SENTRY IN SIGHT?!
'TIS STRANGE INDEED, BUT...

HUH?

ASLEEP...?

THIS LOOKS LIKE...
A SLEEPING SPELL!

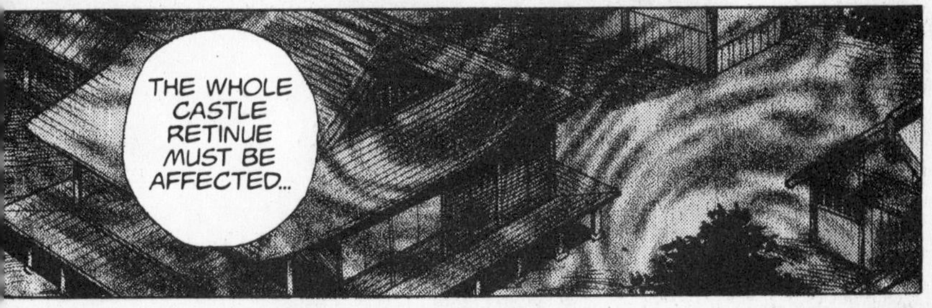
THE WHOLE CASTLE RETINUE MUST BE AFFECTED...

HWOOOOOO
HUHH.
WHAT'S THIS... ?
OUTSIDERS... IN MY DOMAIN... ?!

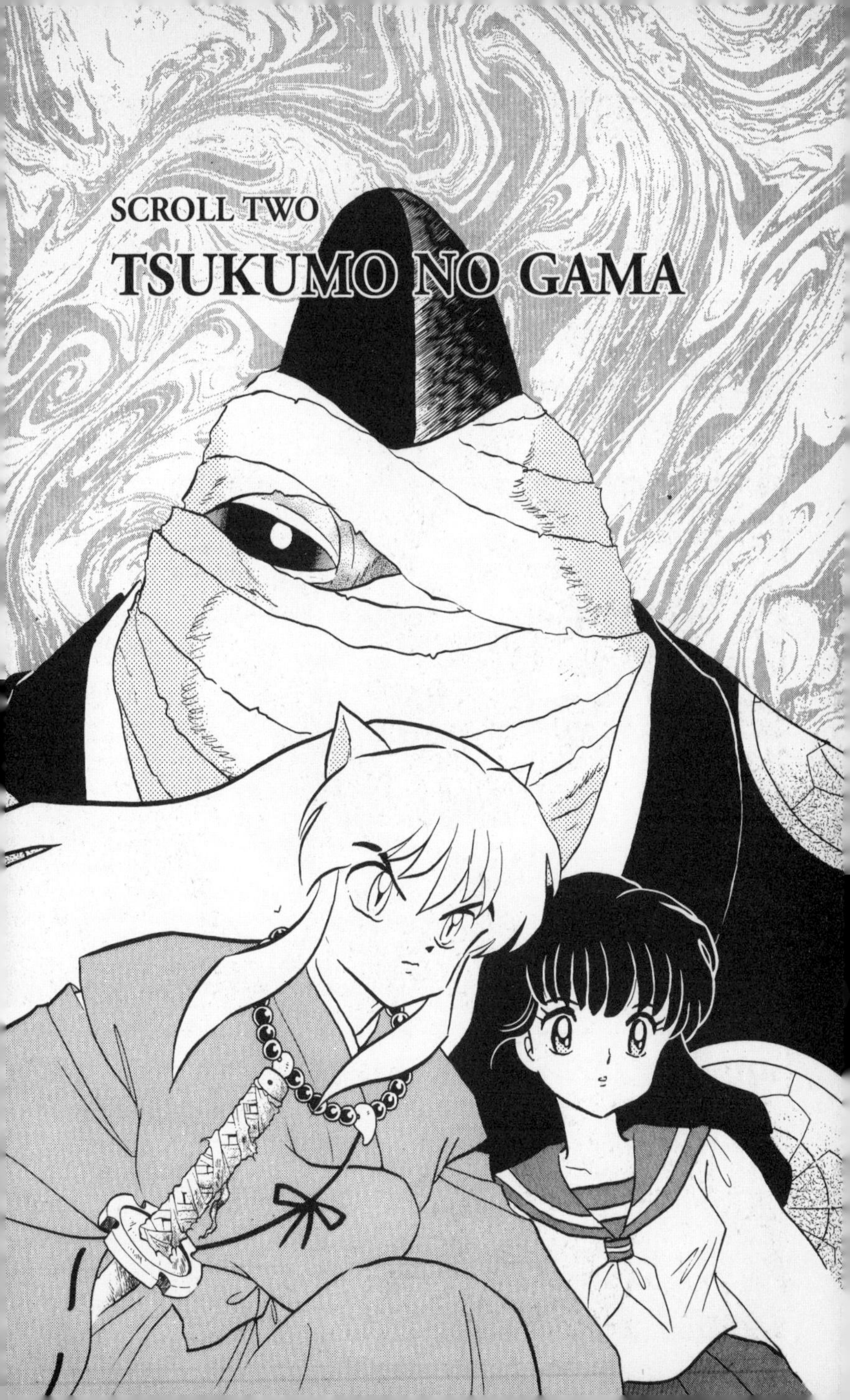
SCROLL TWO
TSUKUMO NO GAMA

SHE IS IN THERE... NEWLY MARRIED INTO THEIR CLAN...

HYUUUUU...

PRINCESS TSUYU... TRAPPED IN THAT CASTLE OF EVIL!

TM TM TM TM

PRINCESS, WHERE ARE YOU?!

NOBUNAGA HAS COME FOR YOU!

ZHOOP
PRINCESS--!
THEY'RE ALL ASLEEP FROM THAT SPELL. AND ANYWAY...
THIS *IS* ENEMY TERRITORY, RIGHT?
SHOULD HE BE *YELLING* LIKE THAT?
...WHAT BETTER WAY TO BRING THAT *DEMON* OUT THAN TO STIR UP A BIT OF A *RUCKUS*, EH?
KRAK
TSUYU!!
ZHOOP

SHNAX
NO...

GAAH!!

OH, PRINCESS...
...BE BRAVE, I'VE...
SHEFF

UH... NOBUNAGA...?
OH, WHERE IS THE FIEND WHO DID THIS TO YOU, PRINCESS?!

OH.
COULD *THIS* BE THE PRINCESS YOU'RE LOOKING FOR?

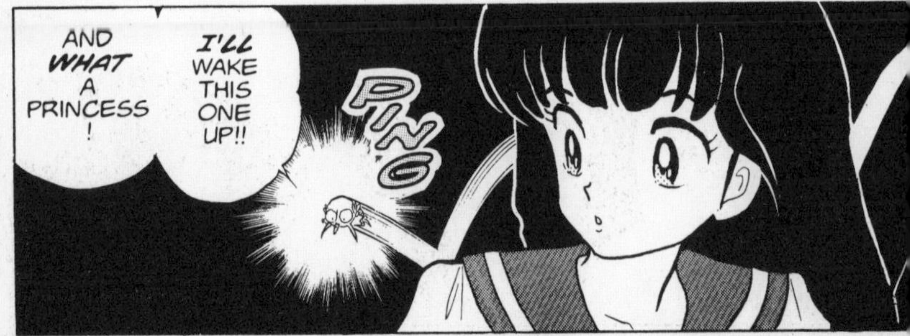
I'LL WAKE THIS ONE UP!!
AND *WHAT* A PRINCESS!
PING

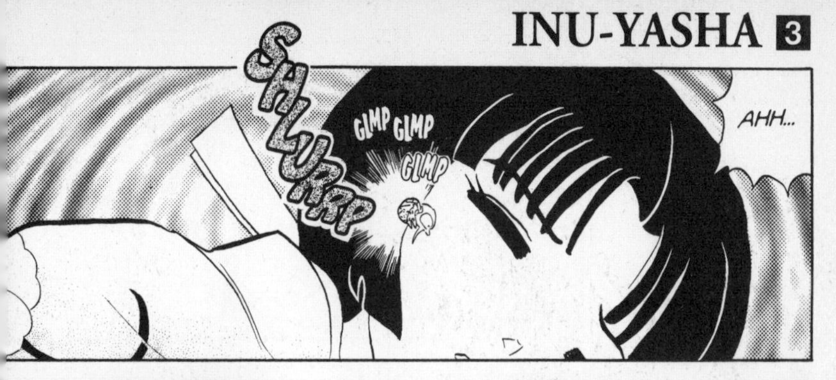
AHH...
SHLURRP
GLMP GLMP
GLMP

WHAP
SQUISH

NN?
GLAG

UH...

YOU RECOGNIZE ME?!
Y-YOUR HIGHNESS...? YOU...
N-NOBUNAGA...?
WHY ARE YOU HERE...?

UH...
HOW COULD I...
EVER FORGET YOU?

...A KIND AND GENTLE CHILDHOOD FRIEND.
TO ME YOU CAN ONLY BE...

OH...PR-PRINCESS... TO...TO...TO REMEMBER THE LIKES OF *ME*...THE YOUNGEST SON OF A RETAINER...I...I...

NO. JUST IDIOCY.
DO YOU SMELL *PUPPY-LOVE*, DOG-BOY?
OH-HO-*HO*!

gasp
gulp

UHH...
YOU ALWAYS MADE ME LAUGH!
...OR SLIP IN HORSE MANURE.
I REMEMBER HOW YOU'D FALL IN THE POND...

PR-PRINCESS...

I WISH I COULD GO BACK TO THOSE DAYS...
Sobb

SOON AFTER THE MARRIAGE, AFTER I'D LEFT OUR DOMAIN...
MY LORD HUSBAND BEGAN ACTING SO STRANGELY...
HYUUUUU...

ONE DAY, HE COLLAPSED AT THE EDGE OF THE GARDEN POND...
HE HAD A HIGH FEVER... AND HE CHANGED.
PLAP

MORE THAN MERELY A CHANGE IN PERSONALITY...
...IT IS AS IF HE BECAME AN ENTIRELY DIFFERENT CREATURE...
PLAP
HEHH... HEHH...

NOBUNAGA...
WHAT AM I TO DO...?
THERE'S NO CHOICE!
YOU MUST COME HOME WITH ME TO THE TAKEDA CLAN!

THE WHISPERS ABOUT YOUR LORD HUSBAND HAVE REACHED EVEN THE TAKEDA DOMAIN.
I HAVE BEEN ORDERED BY *OUR* LORD...

...THAT IF THE WHISPERS PROVE TRUE...
...I AM TO LEAD YOU HOME TO SAFETY!

THEN YOU'VE COME BECAUSE...?
SHA
NO!
EVEN HAD THEY ORDERED ME TO STAY HOME, I WOULD HAVE...

NOBUNAGA...

PRINCESS TSUYU...
I...I...
B-BUMP
B-BUMP
B-BUMP

UM... ON YOUR HEAD...
PAY NO ATTEN-TION TO HIM...!
KEE KEE KEE

MAYBE YOURS IS, BUT *MINE'S* JUST BEGINNING!

PLAP...

KRAK

HEHH...

TRESSSS...

PASSERS...

MY HUSBAND...
WH- WHAT IS THAT...
YOU'LL REGRET THIS...
PLAP...
HUHH...
BWIH
KRUNCH
THOK
HEY!!

SHRAK
NOW--
SHOW YOUR-SELF!
HSSH
OH...
!
TPP

shfff...
PLAP
HEHH...

H-HE'S A...
YEAH...

THAT GLOW... THE JEWEL... !
OH... !
HUHH... HUHH...
GLIMMER...
HUH.
FOR A DEMON WITH A PIECE OF THE JEWEL... HE'S NOT MUCH!
KRAK
THEN HE'LL TAKE THEM... TO HIS GRAVE!
THAT'S TSUKUMO-NO-GAMA, "THE IMMORTAL FROG"--A 300-YEAR-OLD DEMON!
STAY ON YOUR GUARD, INU-YASHA !
ZHA
HE KNOWS SOME THINGS ABOUT FIGHTING !
HSST...

!

NOXIOUS VAPORS!
DON'T BREATHE THEM, KAGOME!
SHOULDN'T YOU BE HELPING INU-YASHA...?
Ka-Hak

HHKH
DMM

HEHH...
PLAAP
!

HSS
BEGONE, DEMON!

HEHH...
MY LITTLE DEW-DROP...
PLAP

LITTLE... HUMAN... FOOL...
BWIIH
!
SHHK

N-
NOBUNAGA...
!
whakk...
HEHH...
PLAP
PLAP
PLAP

DNK

BUT...
I
MUST...
DON'T MOVE!
YOU'RE
WOUNDED!

...SAVE
THE
PRINCESS...
EVEN...
IF I
DIE...
I
MUST...

PRINCESS!

HOW DID YOU KNOW... ?!
YOU... DIDN'T THINK YOU WERE HIDING IT, DID YOU...?
HOW...
I KNOW YOU'RE IN LOVE WITH HER, BUT...
gulp
NOBUNAGA, PLEASE...
HE'S DEAD!
THAT... SLIMY... TOAD!
SHA
WELL.
LOOKS LIKE SOME-BODY'S OKAY AGAIN.

OHHH...

!

MY PRINCESS... ♡

HEHH...

SCROLL THREE
INHERITANCE OF SOULS

HYUUUUUUUU
MY LOVE... MY DEW DROP...
I HAVE BEEN SAVING YOU... ♡
PLAP
gasp...
?!
HHSSSHHHH

HYUUUUUUUU
...
OH...
BURBLE
BURBLE
BWIH

Shllap
RRRAAA
AAAAAAA

WHERE *ARE* YOU, TOAD?!

KOOM!

SLAPP
PLAP
TOO LATE...
HUHH...
UGH
PRINCESS TSUYU!
WELL... THAT ANSWERS THE QUESTION...
...ABOUT THE GIRLS GATHERED FROM ALL OVER THE DOMAIN.

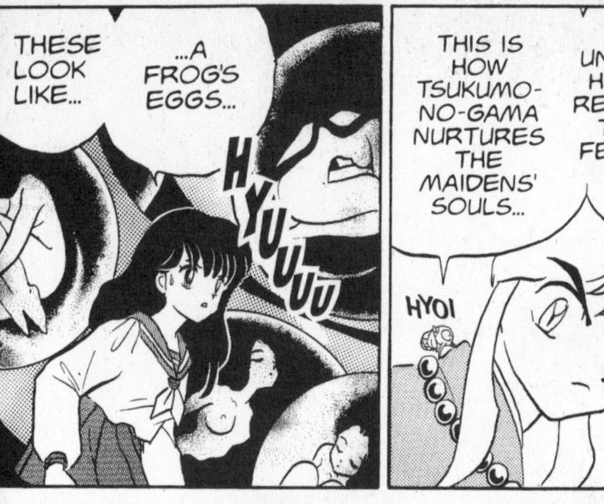
THESE LOOK LIKE...
...A FROG'S EGGS...
HYUUUU

THIS IS HOW TSUKUMO-NO-GAMA NURTURES THE MAIDENS' SOULS...
UNTIL HE'S READY TO FEED.
HYOI

ARE YOU SAYING...
...HE'S GOING TO FEED... ON TSUYU?!!

WITH THE POWER FROM THE JEWEL OF FOUR SOULS...
HEHH...
...THE IMMORTAL FROG TOOK THE LORD'S BODY...AND THUS HIS DOMAIN!
GLIMMER...

SHHH
YOU----!
WOBBLE

HWOO
THE VAPORS!
LOOK OUT--
OUT OF MY WAY!
SHAA
YOU WANT TO RELEASE YOUR VAPORS, TOAD?!

GAAH.
THEN LET'S OPEN YOU !!
SHK
NNNGH.
GUSH
HE DID IT...?!

HEH.
AND NOW THAT YOU'RE OPEN...I'LL TAKE THAT JEWEL.
SSSS
THAT SHOULD PUT AN END TO YOUR FEEDING.
BECAUSE HE'S HELPING HUMANS!
AAAH! THE STEEL-CLEAVING FANG RETURNS TO LIFE!
HUHH...
I AM... DYING...
I NEED... A SOUL...
A SOUL...
BURBLE BURBLE BURBLE

SHURU
SHURU SHURU
WHAT?
MY GIRLS ARE GOOD TO ME... ♡
PLORP
PLAP
HEHH...
SHHRRR SHHRRR
THE MORE YOU SLICE, THE MORE I'LL DEVOUR...
COME! SLICE ME AGAIN...
YOU... SLIMY...
HE'S... HEALED!
RRRIB-BIT

GLUH
HUHH
HUHH

BLORB
GLGG
GLGG
PRINCESS
!
SHLOK
EHH...
?

OH...
gasp

NOBUNAGA...!

NOH...
OH,
PRINCESS...

PRINCESS...
TSUYU...
B-BUMP
B-BUMP
B-BUMP

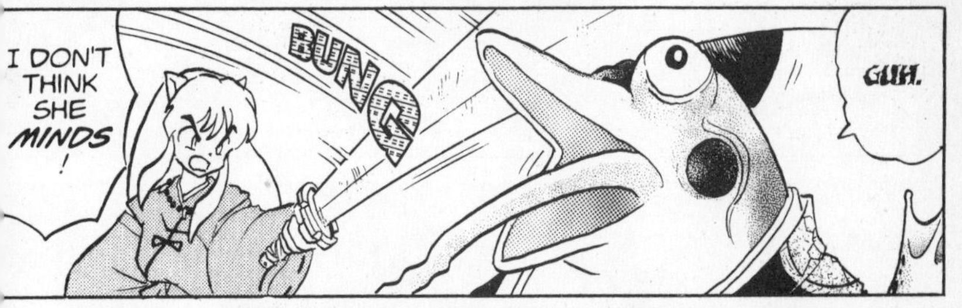

WHO... WHO...?

WHAT...?

PLAP

PLAP

...

OBBLE

WOBBLE OBBLE

MY...

PRINCESS...

HUH. DON'T EVEN TRY THAT OLD TRICK, TOAD!
...

HYUUUUU
DID I...
DID I DO THIS...?

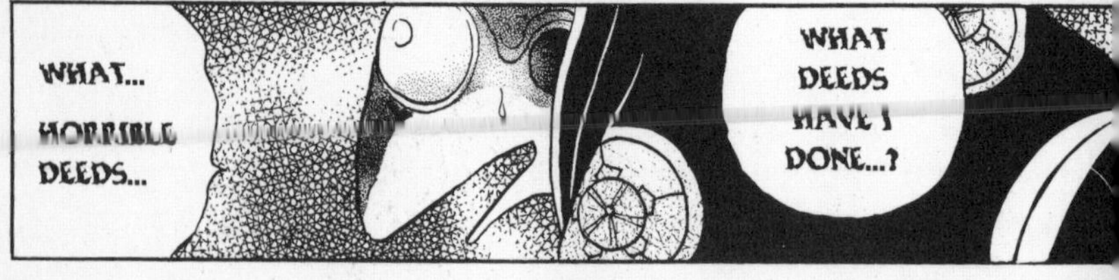
WHAT DEEDS HAVE I DONE...?
WHAT... HORRIBLE DEEDS...

WHEN THAT DEMON FIRST POSSESSED ME...I RETAINED MY HUMAN CONSCIOUSNESS...
THEN... I LOST EVEN THAT...

ARE YOU THE REAL LORD...?
I AM...

WAIT... COULD IT BE...?

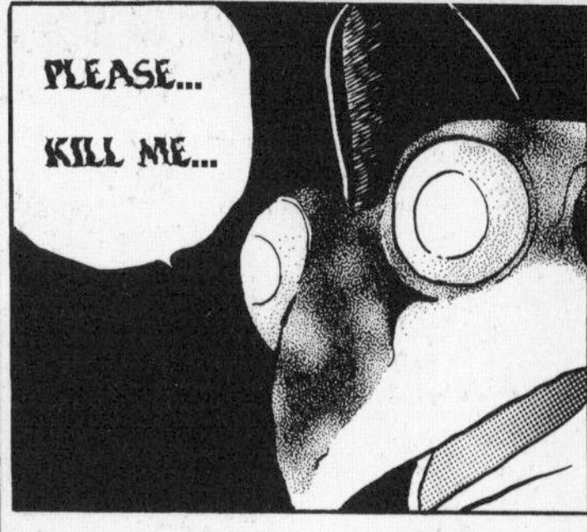
PLEASE...
KILL ME...

HE'S STILL ALIVE...
INSIDE THAT HORRIBLE... THING!!

BUT...

...
MY LORD...

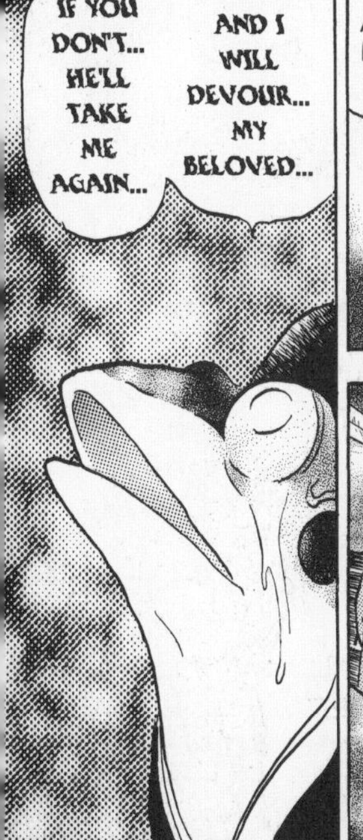
AND I WILL DEVOUR... MY BELOVED...
IF YOU DON'T... HE'LL TAKE ME AGAIN...

YOU'D... YOU'D REALLY...?
BEFORE THAT CAN HAPPEN, YOU MUST KILL ME...AND THUS HIM, AS WELL.

HOW VERY NOBLE. I ADMIRE YOUR SACRIFICE.
AND SO, WITHOUT FURTHER ADO...
GYUU
HUH... ?!

INU-YASHA, WAIT !!
YOU CAN'T SIMPLY *KILL* HIM!

THERE'S A *MAN* IN THERE!
AND A GOOD ONE, IT SOUNDS LIKE!

BUT HOW LONG CAN THAT MAN LAST... AGAINST THE DEMON ?
WE CAN SAVE HIM!
SIGH

SHUT *UP*! ALL OF YOU!
HE *TOLD* ME TO KILL HIM!

SAVE YOUR SENTI-MENTALITY!
SHHSSH
FWK
INU-YASHA...!
SHHH
SHHHH
SHHHH

OH...
...
SSSS
FEH!
I SHOULD'VE KILLED HIM WHEN I FIRST MEANT TO!
TK TK
HE COULDN'T DO IT...
Phew...
INU-YASHA...

HUH
?
SO. WHAT DO YOU PLAN TO DO WITH HIM?

NOW *YOU* THINK OF A WAY TO TAKE CARE OF HIM!
YOU TOLD ME NOT TO KILL HIM.

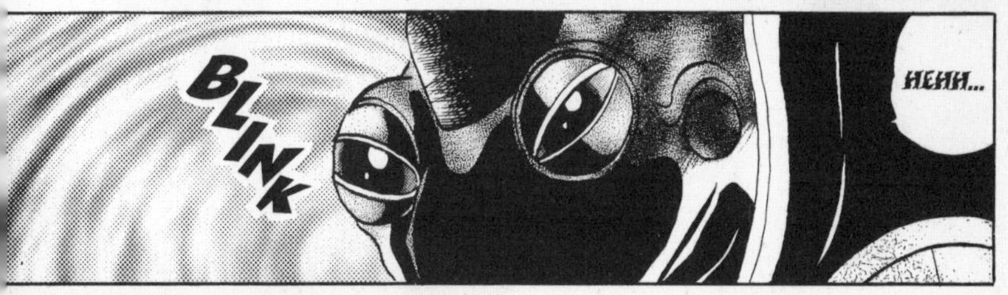
HEHH...
BLINK

INU-YASHA !!
SHMP
ZZHH

!
THWK

GOING TO FINISH ME OFF... WERE YOU?
HEHH...
HEHH...
FFFSSHH

THE DEMON HAS TAKEN HIM AGAIN...
THE LORD...

MYŌGA... WHAT...?
KAGOME!

I'LL BEGIN WITH YOU... PRETTY MAIDEN...
MY TURN NOW...
PLAP...

HURRY!
THEN TELL ME...
I HAVE AN IDEA TO DRIVE TSUKUMO-NO-GAMA FROM THE LORD'S BODY.
THERE MIGHT BE A WAY...
PLAAP...

YES!
WHAT ELSE HAVE WE GOT?!
WILL YOU GAMBLE?!
IT MAY NOT WORK...

SCROLL FOUR
PLEA FOR MERCY

...AND LEAVE US ALIVE, TOO?!
A WAY THAT'LL LEAVE HIM ALIVE...
AND TOADS ARE VULNERABLE TO HEAT.
HE MAY BE A DEMON TOAD, BUT HE'S STILL A TOAD.
LOOK.
JUST DRENCH HIM WITH BOILING WATER!
DON'T YOU GET IT?
BOILING WATER?!

WOW. GREAT.
WELL... ?
THE HEAT WILL BE UNBEARABLE TO HIS TOAD-SELF AND HE'LL JUMP RIGHT OUT!

HUHH
EXCEPT HOW IN THE HECK AM I GONNA GET BOILING WATER IN THIS DUNGEON?!

HENH.
NO! LEMME GO!!
SHRRRRRRRR

OH, THANKS VERY MUCH!
OKAY, SO USE BOILING OIL INSTEAD!

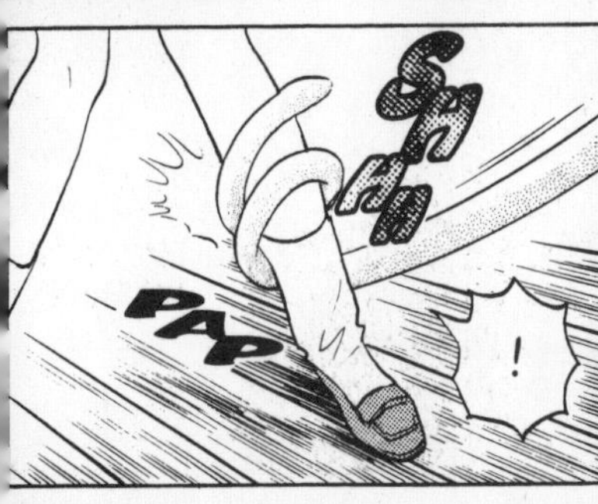
SHH
!
PAP

GLUHH.

GYNG

PLEASE, MY LORD, *NO!*

N... *NO...* !

NGUH

DMF

RUN WHILE I'M HOLDING HIM, KAGOME...

RUN !!

BATA FAPA

N- NOBU... NAGA...

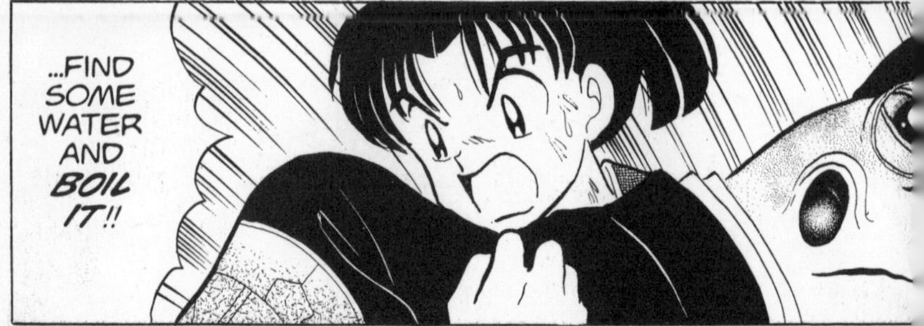

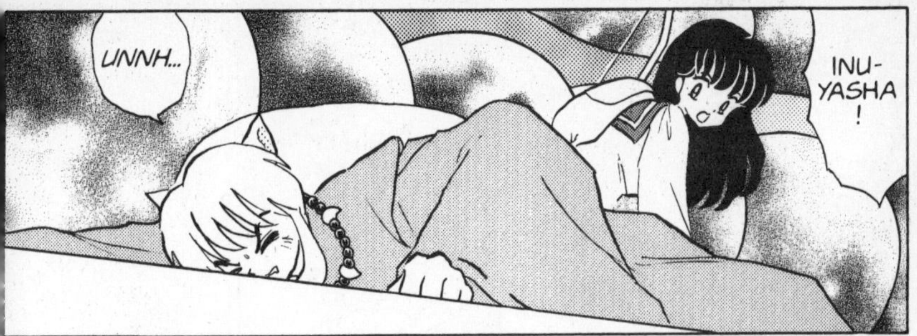
INU-YASHA!
UNNH...

DON'T GET UP... YOU'RE HURT...
NGH...

...EVERY STUPID, SOFT, SENTI-MENTAL WORD!
I'VE HEARD YOU TALKING...

BUT I S'POSE I'M THE STUPIDEST AND SOFTEST OF YOU ALL... LETTING THAT **FROG** MAKE A FOOL OF ME...
HUH!

WHA...
SHHH...
OUT OF MY **WAY**, NOBUNAGA...

WILL YOUR "FANG" KILL A HUMAN ?!

GET OUT OF THE WAY OR I'LL CLEAVE YOU BOTH!

THE LORD IS TRAPPED WITHIN THIS DEMON FORM--BUT STILL ALIVE!
SHEATH YOUR BLADE!
SHUT UP !!

I WILL NOT MOVE.
DAMN IT ALL!
NO...

EVEN IF HE WERE A COMMONER!
I'D SAY THE SAME...
IF THERE IS ANY HOPE AT ALL TO SAVE HIM, I CANNOT STAND BY AND WATCH AN INNOCENT LORD BE SLAIN!

NOBUNAGA...

OH, NOBUNAGA...

A HARD WORLD MAY LAUGH AT MY NAIVETÉ...
THESE ARE BLOODY TIMES...
BUT I STILL *BELIEVE*...

WH...?
ALL RIGHT.

...DON'T *BELIEVE* IN *KILLING*!
I SIMPLY...

GO AHEAD AND BEAT THIS FROG WITH YOUR PRETTY IDEALS.

I'M NOT LIFTING A FINGER FOR ANY OF YOU.

HEHH.

WE *WILL*... YOU'LL *SEE*... WE...

GYNG
K-KAGOME... HURRY...!

COME WITH ME, PRINCESS!
WHAT...?

WE NEED HEAT!
D'YOU HAVE A FIRE?
D'YOU HAVE ANY TORCHES?!
TM TM TM

HIYOSHIMARU...
SKRATTLE
BEGONE, MAMMAL!
!
SHNK

HUH ?!
pff...
HE'S COMING!
TM TM
COME BACK, PRETTIES...
HEHH...
PLEP

FIRE ?!
GOOD GOING, LI'L MONKEY...

THAT'S...
...REALLY... REALLY... SMALL...
FFZ FFZ
SKRICH SKRICH

SHHP
RRAK
!
OH...
HENH.
DOMP
KLATTA KLATTA

EH?

DOOM

INU... YASHA...?

I LET YOU HAVE YOUR SAY. NOW IT'S TIME TO DROP THE FOOLISHNESS.
KRRAK
THAT'S IT.

HOW...CAN YOU CALL IT...
...FOOLISHNESS...?
ZH ZH
...
HAIR SPRAY...
THAT'S IT!
THAT'S THE ANSWER!
TO THE DEATH!!
SHAA
!
VWIP

INU-YASHA... *SIT!!*

WHAT?!

GYAA!

WOOMP

PSSHHH...

DMF

WHAT *MAGIC*--?!

hyeeeee
BWMM
I...I DID IT!
SSHHHHHH...
Pff...
YOU DON'T HAVE TO REMIND ME!
THE SHIKON JEWEL...!
INU-YASHA...

CLAWS OF STEEL!!

THE LORD IS FREE... AND UNHURT!
HHHSSHHHH
NNNH...
HOW CAN I THANK YOU?
GNYUU
AND ALL BECAUSE *YOU* WERE COMPASSIONATE ENOUGH...
...TO *WAIT* UNTIL KAGOME COULD DRIVE THE TOAD FROM HIS BODY!

OH, NOBUNAGA...
SHA...
OH, YOUR HIGHNESS...
MY DEW-DROP!
THANK YOU FOR SAVING MY HUSBAND!
I AM SO SORRY TO HAVE GIVEN YOU SUCH GRIEF.
HOW SWEET TO SEE YOUR FACE AGAIN...
MY DARLING...
LOOKS LIKE A NICE GUY... AS FEUDAL LORDS GO...

hssh...
SO THE TOAD-DEMON'S GONE, THE WOMEN ARE SAVED, AND THE LAND IS FREE...
DOES THAT QUALIFY AS "HAPPILY EVER AFTER"?

HEY...
CAN'T YOU EVEN MANAGE A WEAK SMILE, NOBUNAGA?

hssh...

YOU'RE RIGHT...
I'M A FOOL...

heh...

HE NEARLY GETS HIMSELF KILLED...TO SAVE THE LIFE OF HIS RIVAL IN LOVE!
WHAT DO YOU EXPECT FROM A FOOLISH LITTLE PUP?
RRK

YEAH.

BUT YOUR FOLLY SAVED A MAN'S LIFE, DIDN'T IT?

THAT'S SOME-THING, I GUESS.

THANK YOU...FOR SAYING SO.

AND NOW THAT WE'VE RESTED...

LET'S *GO*!

huff.

HUH?

"GO"...? BUT...

NOBUNAGA...

YOU HAVE TROUBLE WITH CLIFFS, DON'T YOU?

OKAY, SO MAYBE HE *IS* A FOOL...

KALAK...

SCROLL FIVE

MASK OF FLESH

TWITWI...

MUSASHI'S DOMAIN

KAGOME AND INU-YASHA HAVE RETURNED, YOU SAY?

YOU WON'T RUN OUT ON *ME*!
VVVZZZZZZ
...I'LL BE RIGHT *BACK*!
I *TOLD* YOU...
WHAT ABOUT MY *EXAMS*?!
I'M TRYING TO GET INTO A GOOD HIGH SCHOOL!
WHAT ABOUT THE SHIKON JEWEL ?!
ZMP
SSHHP
IF I BLOW THE *ENTRANCE EXAMS*, I CAN JUST *FORGET* IT!
MY ATTENDANCE RECORD ALREADY SUCKS ROYALLY, THANKS TO YOU!

UM... MAY I ASK WHAT YOU'RE DOING ?
FRAK
VWOOM
HYAH...
IF THIS... MAGIC **WELL** GETS PLUGGED UP...
...YOU'LL NEVER... GET BACK HOME... WILL YOU?

I'LL BE BACK IN THREE DAYS!

AND DON'T YOU *DARE* COME AFTER ME!

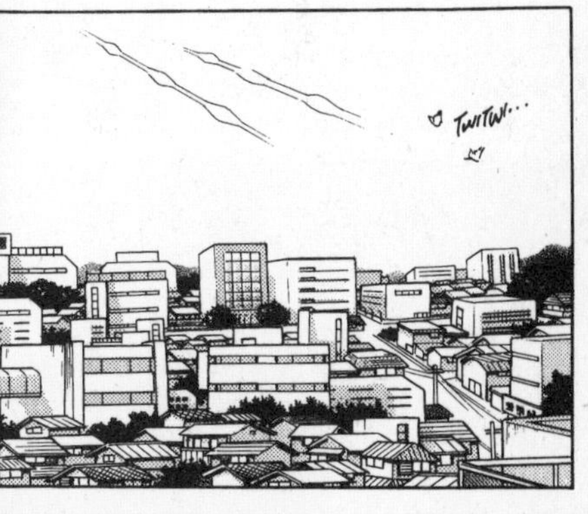

FEAR NOT!
THIS SPELL HAS BEEN PASSED DOWN FROM MASTER TO MASTER OF THE SUNSET SHRINE FOR GENERA-TIONS...

BUT YOU'VE BEEN DOING IT FOR THREE DAYS NOW... AND SIS STILL HASN'T COME BACK!
COOOOME... HOOOOME... COOOOME... HOOOME... COOOME...
pff
Pff

HWOOM
TOUCH-DOWN!

HUH?
Pff
Pff

AND NOW...
BLOOSH
THE SACRA-MENTAL SAKE!

MY SPELL ***WORKED***!

KAGOME! IT'S YOU!

DON'T GET ME STARTED...

DRIP DRIP

IT'S SAID TO HAVE SURVIVED FROM THE ERA OF WARRING STATES...
...AND TO BE INDESTRUCTIBLE, EVEN BY FIRE.

ANYONE WHO ATTEMPTS TO DESTROY IT...OR EVEN DEFACE IT...WILL MEET A STRANGE DEMISE.
OF COURSE, I DON'T BELIEVE SUCH THINGS... BUT STILL...
hsssh...
Higurashi Shrine
WELL...

DEAR ME...
THIS PLACE IS AS SPOOKY AS...

CHKA CHKA CHKA

Y'MEAN YOU DIDN'T BRING THAT DOG-GUY BACK WITH YOU?

AM I *STUPID*?

DO YOU KNOW WHAT I WENT THROUGH TO GET *RID* OF HIM?!

KAGOME!

YOUR UNIFORM'S DRY!

THANKS, MOM!

WHA...?

HUH?

IZZAT A CUSTOMER...?

Wssh...

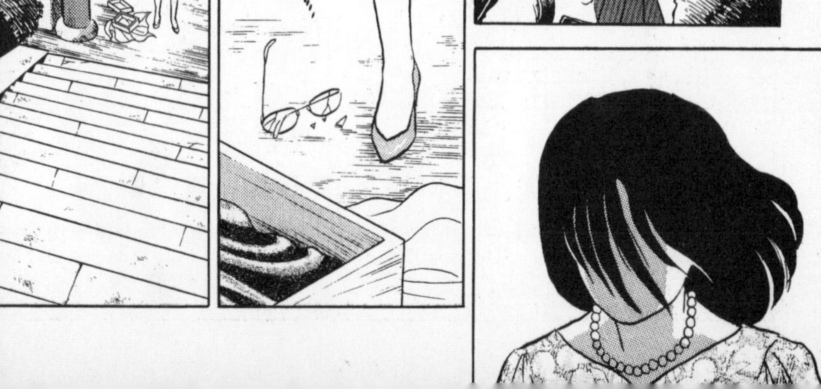

hwsh...

GASP
BRRR

SH-SHE SCARES ME...
PSST
SHH!
DON'T BE RUDE, SOTA!
BUT...SHE SCARES ME TOO...WITH THAT FACE LIKE A *NOH* MASK...
AND THOS
SCARS

hssh...

IT IS HER REAL FACE...ISN'T IT...?

VWPP

hss...

C-C'MON, SIS, LET'S GO!
Y... YEAH.

I THOUGHT I...FELT SOMETHING WEIRD...
BUT... THERE CAN'T BE ANY DEMONS HERE... CAN THERE?

...

G'MORNING!
KAGOME!
ARE YOU SURE YOU OUGHTTA BE BACK IN SCHOO SO SOON?
YOUR GRAMPA SAID YOU SPRAINED YOUR BACK...
AND BEFORE THAT YOU WERE IN THE HOSPITAL FOR DIABETES TESTS... AND...
YOU'VE BEEN ABSENT SO MUCH WE GOT WORRIED AND CALLED YOUR PLACE.
HUH?

HOW CAN YOU LIVE THAT LONG...
...AND NOT EVEN LEARN HOW TO TELL A GOOD LIE?!
YEAH, THAT'S IT... LEUKEMIA!
HIGURASHI...
SKW!!
BACK ON YOUR FEET SO SOON?
HUH...?
WOW
IT'S HOJO... FROM B CLASS!
IT MUST HAVE BEEN AWFUL! HAVING GOUT AT SUCH A YOUNG AGE, I MEAN!
HHHHSSSS...
I'LL KILL HIM... I'LL KILL HIM...
I DON'T...
...KNOW ANY WAY TO HELP, BUT...

SHIATSU SANDALS!
WEAR 'EM!
CHIRIRIN
LATER!

UHH...

I DUNNO...

I GUESS...

A GUY WHO'S NOT TOO WILD...

...NOT TOO FULL OF HIM-SELF...

...NOT TOO ANGRY...

...NOT TOO STUB-BORN...

...AND IS ALWAYS UNDER-STANDING.

IN SHORT...

FEH.

...ANY GUY WHO'S THE EXACT **OPPOSITE** OF INU-YASHA!

STOP MOPING ABOUT, INU-YASHA! GO GATHER SOME RUMORS OF THE SHIKON JEWEL, OR SOMETHING.

THROB THROB

GET OFF MY BACK!

IT'S STILL **KILLING** ME AFTER THOSE EIGHT "SITS" IN A ROW!

UHHH... I'M SO... TOTALLY... BURNT OUT...
I'M PROBABLY GONNA GET SICK...
AND THERE ARE STILL FOUR SHARDS OF THE SHIKON JEWEL TO GO...

I WONDER HOW LONG...
I CAN KEEP UP THIS "DOUBLE LIFE"...

SIGH...

YAAUGH!!
I'VE GOT TO STUDY!
I GOT MY WORST SUBJECT COMING UP TOMORROW!
POP
MATH III

hee
hee
hee
hee
hee...

SCROLL SIX

THE BROKEN BODY

HYUUUU...

TPP...
ZZZ

...THAT THE JEWEL OF SOULS...STILL EXISTS...
OH, SO HAPPY...
THPP...

MONO

HYUUUUU...

UMAO...I DON'T KNOW WHY... BUT THIS PLACE GIVES ME THE CREEPS...

VMMMM...

STRANGE THINGS HAPPEN IN THIS NEIGHBORHOOD, SHIKAKO...

LIKE THE GHOST OF THAT WOMAN WHO DIED IN THAT HIT-AND-RUN...

AAA, DON'T *TELL* ME!

THUDDDD
SKREEEE
EEEEEE!
WHA... ?
ZH ZH ZH ZH ZH
DMF

SHLP...
ggg...

SHUU...
gg gg...
KRAK

SHOOP
WHAT HAPPENED...? THOUGHT I HEARD...

...
tk tk tk tk tk

WHAT... WHAT... WHAT...
PSSHHH

gg gg...

GYAAAHHH...
I'VE HARDLY GOT ANY STUDYING DONE!

BRRRRR
2 A.M. ?!
GOMP

YOU KNOW, M'LORD...

...YOU DON'T LOOK HAPPY.

Sigh

SHUT UP, FLEA.

GET BACK HERE, KAGOME...

WITHOUT YOU TO PICK ON...WHAT'S THE POINT OF GETTING UP?

EXAM DAY...

BRRRRING

FREE AT LAST!

I WISH I WAS YOU, KAGOME.

YOU'RE *ALWAYS* IN THE TOP 30 FOR THE WHOLE SCHOOL.

heh heh heh

WELL, I DON'T KNOW ABOUT THAT MATH TEST...

HIGURASHI!

HUH?

...
KAGOME! IT'S HOJO!

HOW ARE YOU FEELING ?
KREE

UM... HERE. FOR YOU...

DO YOU LIKE MOVIES ?
SAY, HIGURASHI...

YAH...
YOU STEP ON IT.
IT'S GOOD FOR YOUR HEALTH.

A...FOOT MASSAGER... ?

HUH... ?

I WAS WONDERING IF WE COULD GO TOGETHER SOMETIME.
JUST THE TWO OF US...
UH...
DON'T TELL ME...
...HE'S ASKING ME OUT...?

C'MON, KAGOME? ANSWER HIM!
ARE YOU GOING OR NOT ?!

YOU'VE GOTTA GO!
I MEAN YOU'VE NEVER HAD A DATE, HAVE YOU?
HEY!
I HAVE SO HAD DATES!
I... I...

I HAVEN'T...!

UH... SURE... I GUESS.
REALLY ?!

THEN LET'S MAKE IT THIS SATURDAY!
PROMISE!
WHA...
ch-ching

I CAN'T BE MAKING DATES...
AARGH! I HAVE TO GO BACK THERE-- THE FEUDAL AGE!

M- ME ?
MISS HIGURASHI!
MAY I SEE YOU?

MUH...
MAKE-UP EXAM... ?!
Faculty Office

I'M SURE IT'S BEEN A DIFFICULT FEW WEEKS, WHAT WITH THE BERI-BERI AND THE RHEUMATISM AND ALL...
BUT YOU CAN MAKE IT UP ON SATURDAY.
'FRAID SO.
EXAMS! Do Not Enter!
ZEEH ZEEH ZEEH
MATH...
I FAILED... ?!

KLANG KLANG KLANG
WH- WHAT AM I GONNA DO...?
THAT'S ONLY THREE DAYS AWAY!!
MAKE IT UP ON SATURDAY... ?!
BARRRA
KRIKKKLE
HSSSHHH...
SOME-THING... EVIL... ?!
WHAT...?! THAT CHILL...!

BWA...
INU-YASHA...?!
WE'RE GOING HOME, KAGOME.
TNG
WHAT TIMING, INU-YASHA!
I WANTED TO SEE YOU!!
YOU...
YOU DID...?
NOT THAT I...*CARE* WHAT YOU WANT...

LOOK, MATH IS HARD ENOUGH FOR ME ALREADY...
YOU'RE AN IDIOT!!
...WITHOUT TRYING TO STUDY IT IN THE MIDDLE AGES!
WHAT?! THREE MORE DAYS?!

EVEN... AFTER PLEADING... AFTER BEGGING...?
ABSO-LUTELY NOT.
PLEASE, INU-YASHA! DON'T BE CRUEL!
NO.
IF I BLOW THE MAKE-UP IT'LL RUIN MY GRADE P--

WHAT...?
hssst

Sigh

HRRR

GULP

THEN WHAT ARE YOU GONNA DO ABOUT MY *FUTURE*?!

WHA... WHA...
MAYBE ALL *YOU* CARE ABOUT IS YOUR STUPID *JEWEL*--
--BUT *I'VE* GOT A LIFE IN *THIS* WORLD TOO, Y'KNOW!!

SHE'S... CRYING...
BUT I DIDN'T MEAN TO...TO MAKE HER...
B-BMP B-BMP B-BMP

KAGOME... LISTEN...
WILL YOU JUST GO AWAY? JUST...

HEY, WHAT DID I EVER DO TO *YOU*?!

...GO!!
BOOT

MORONNNN...
Pff

HYUUUU...

DNK
ST-STOP IT...
STOP IT... PLEASE!

SO, OLD MAN. YOU'RE PRETTY LOADED AFTER ALL, HUH?

'SNOT ALL! HA!
OH, GOSH, HIS LI'L GLASSES BROKE!
SNORT
"ST-STOP IT... STOP IT... PLEASE!" HA HA!
DMP
TMP

...ALL BROKEN...
THIS BODY... NOT GOOD NOW...
HUH?
GLSH...
SSHHH
BWOK...

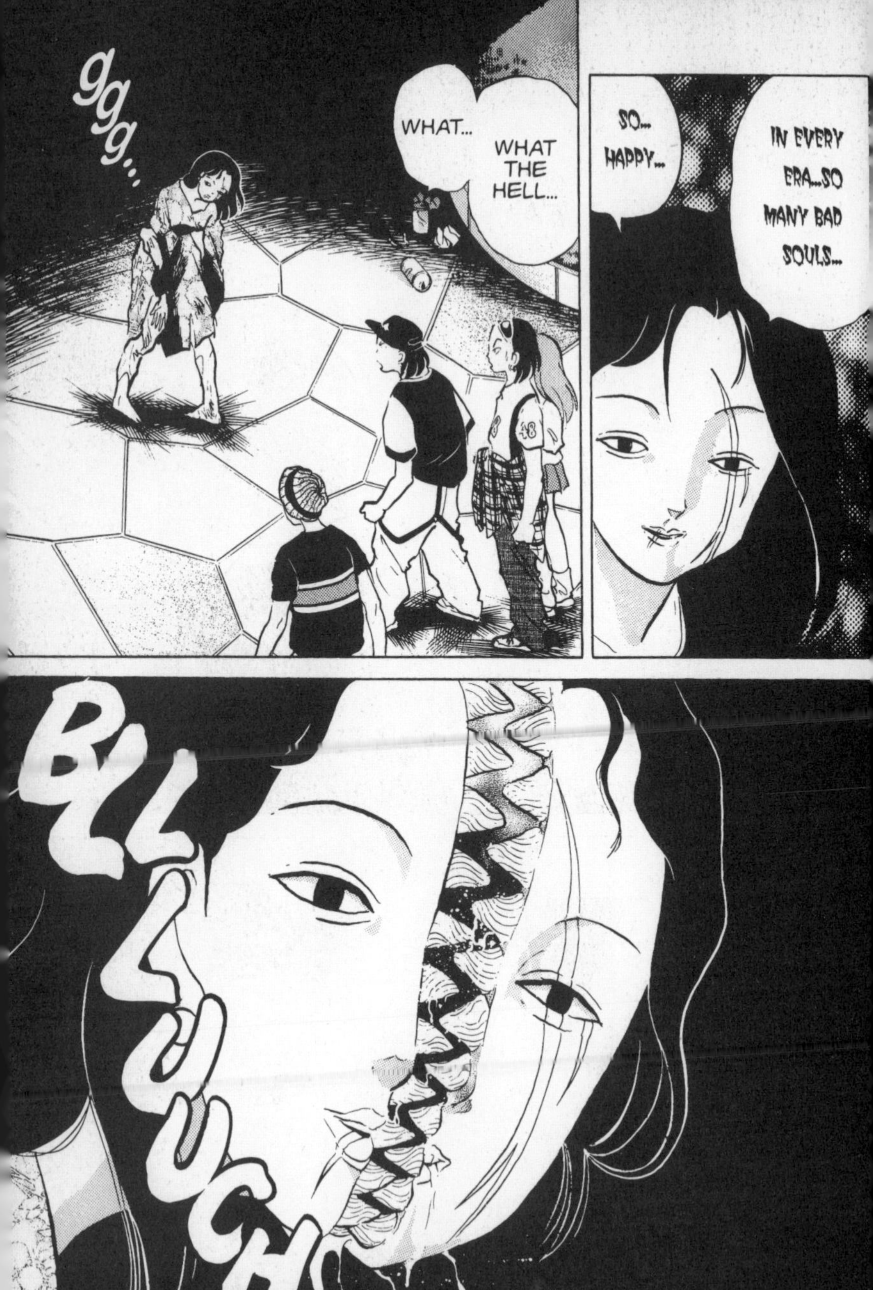
IN EVERY ERA...SO MANY BAD SOULS...
SO... HAPPY...
WHAT...
WHAT THE HELL...
ggg...
BLLUUCH!

BLK

HSSH

UH...!

gggg...

TO TAKE THE JEWEL...

I NEED A STRONGER BODY...

MSH MSH

fmp

SPT SPT

...NEED MORE BAD SOULS...

SHUWOP
KRAK
KRAK
KRAK

EEEEEEE!!
HHHSSSS
NOOOOO!!
N...

HYUUU...

I WOULDN'T TAKE YOU BACK IF YOU BEGGED ME!

DAMN YOU, KAGOME.

SCROLL SEVEN

FACE OFF

HEY, DID YOU HEAR?

ABOUT LAST NIGHT, IN THE PARK?

3-A

A *MURDER*...?

OOOHHH... WHAT HAPPENED?

...

THIS BUNCH OF JUNIOR-HIGH KIDS WERE OUT MUGGING PEOPLE, BUT...WELL...

THEY HAVEN'T FOUND THE BODIES.

NOTHING LEFT BUT SOME SCRAPS OF CLOTHES IN A SEA OF BLOOD...

SHE... SHE ATE THEM ALL.
A WOMAN WITH A FACE LIKE A NOH MASK, WHOSE NECK GREW AND GREW AND...
I SWEAR THAT'S HOW IT HAPPENED.
48
48
BUT WHEN THEY SEARCHED THE PARK...
YOU'RE KIDDING.
THIS GUY WAS DRUNK, RIGHT?
...WITH-OUT A HEAD.
THEY FOUND THE BODY OF SOME UNKNOWN WOMAN...

SHH...
I DON'T LIKE IT...
DO NOT CROSS
"A WOMAN WITH A FACE LIKE A NOH MASK, WHOSE NECK GREW AND GREW..."
IT SOUNDS LIKE A DEMON...
I DON'T WANT TO BELIEVE IT, BUT...
...MAYBE I SHOULD GET INU-YASHA...
WOGGA
WOGGA
WOGGA
WHAT AM I *THINKING* ?!

NO WAY I'LL GET ANY STUDYING DONE WITH HIM AROUND.
THINK MATH EXAM, MATH EXAM...
NOW WHERE'S THAT STUDY GUIDE...?

HUH?
FWUMP
WHAT?
MATH
ENGLISH
History
History

WHERE IS IT?!
WHERE COULD IT GO?!
Science

NNNHH...
High School
MATHEMATICS
Quick Solutions to All Problems
High School MATHE
$\frac{x}{2}-1<\frac{3x+5}{4}$
WHAT KIND OF SPELL IS THIS...?

WHAT WRITINGS DO YOU HAVE THERE, LORD INU-YASHA?
poing
I HAVE NO CLUE.
I FOUND IT IN KAGOME'S ROOM.

FRIDAY...

WHAT? GRAMPA... IN THE HOSPITAL?!

IT'S JUST A LITTLE FOOD POISON-ING...

BUT BECAUSE OF HIS AGE, I'LL BE STAYING WITH HIM IN THE HOSPITAL TONIGHT.

HSHH...

DON'T BE SUCH A WUSS.
BUT I'M SCARED...

ARE'NT YOU TOO OLD FOR THAT?
OH, COME ON, SOTA...
CAN I SLEEP WITH YOU TONIGHT...?
HEY, GOME...?

BUT... BUT YOU HEARD ABOUT THE PARK...

DON'T YOU REMEMBER?
THAT LADY WE SAW...

HOW DOES THAT...
"A WOMAN WITH A FACE LIKE A NOH MASK..."
...AFFECT YOU?

OH...
...WITH THE FACE LIKE A MASK...
THAT WOMAN...
KREEK
SHMP SHMP
COULD SHE... COULD SHE HAVE BEEN...?
"...WHOSE NECK GREW AND GREW...
...AND ATE THEM ALL."

KSHH
!

TING
TING

THE *MASK*...
TING

SHLP...
UH...
PTT...

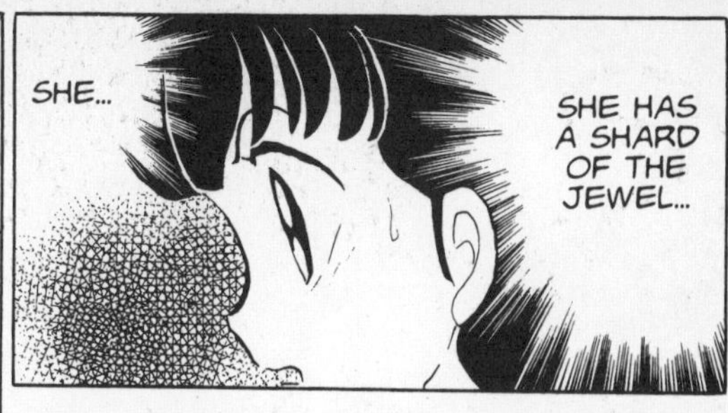
SHE...
SHE HAS A SHARD OF THE JEWEL...

NEED...
...A BETTER... BODY...
GLINT

SHE KNOWS...

!
GIVE ME...
THE SHARDS...

gng
gng
gng

ZZHH
GIVVVVE... THEMMM...
PUH
NO!!
GHH
KKKH

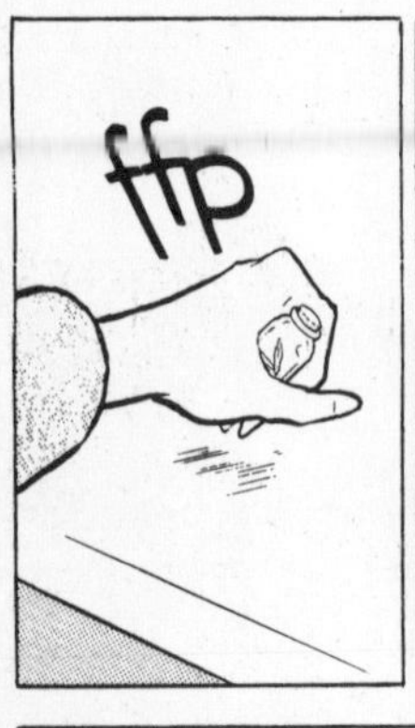

I'VE GOT TO CALL TO INU-YASHA.
INU-YASHA...
TMTMTM

HSS...

QUIT SCREAMING! IT'S JUST A CUT, OKAY?!
KAGOME... YOU'RE BLEEDING!

...
PLP...

RUN, SOTA! HURRY!
thp thp
SHK SHK

EEK!
SHFF

YAAA!
ZHZH
gng
DINK

SOTA...
PLUP
KA...
KA...
KAGOME...
?

THAT MONSTER WANTS THESE SHARDS...

RIPRIP
DMF

UGH...
SHH
SHE'LL FOLLOW *ME* IF I RUN...

GIVVVE... THEMMM.
ZMP

B-BY MYSELF ?!
HUH ?

RUN TO THE WELL !
SOTA !
KAGOME !
CALL FOR INU-YASHA !

HE'LL BE HERE !
DON'T SAY IT'S FOR ME! TELL HIM THERE'S A SHARD OF THE JEWEL AT STAKE!

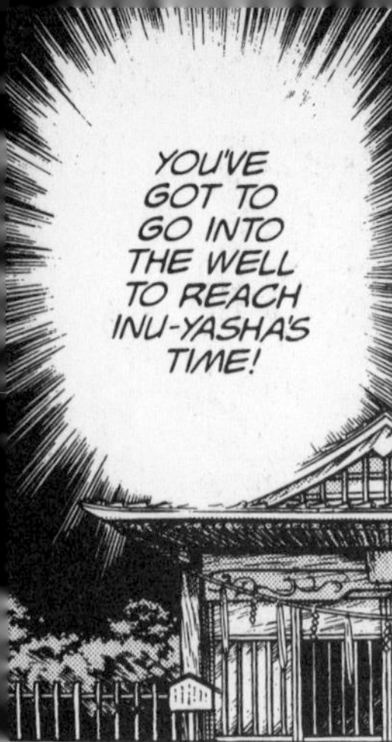
YOU'VE GOT TO GO INTO THE WELL TO REACH INU-YASHA'S TIME!

DMDMDMDMDM

TAKE A DEEP BREATH... AND JUMP IN!
HU-HA HU-HA

INU...
...YAAAAAAAA--
FWA

SHOMP

NNNNG

HUH... ?
NYOWW
I DIDN'T GO THROUGH... ?

KA-GOOOOOO-ME !!!
WAAAAH!!

huff
huff
huff
HYUUUUUUUUUUU...
gg...
HURRY...
HURRY, INU-YASHA...

KFF
KFF

OPEN, PLEASE !
PLEASE...
KFF

...SHE'S IN *TROUBLE* !!
MY SISTER...

PFFAUOOO

UH...

SHA

SCROLL EIGHT
I'LL HELP YOU, BUT...

HYOOOOOOO...
WE GOTTA FIND HER FAST...
OR SHE COULD DIE!
I'M HERE NOW, BOY... NOTHING WILL HAPPEN TO HER.
FWOO
I COULDN'T GET THROUGH THE WELL...
BUT HOW'D YOU KNOW...?
I HAVE A SHARP NOSE.
YOU HAVE A DROP OF KAGOME'S BLOOD ON YOUR HAND, DON'T YOU?

I'LL FIND HER... AND SAVE HER!!
WHEREVER YOUR SISTER IS...

HOW COME HE ALWAYS ACTS SO DIFFERENT FROM WHAT SHE SAYS...?

FOR AN ARROGANT, SELFISH, STUBBORN...
OH, YEAH, INU-YASHA'S GREAT...
...MISOGYNIST, VIOLENT, ANGRY...

...STUPID, NARROW-MINDED, DOG-BREATHED JERK!

...

I KNOW I CAN TRUST HIM!
HE'S ALWAYS GOOD...

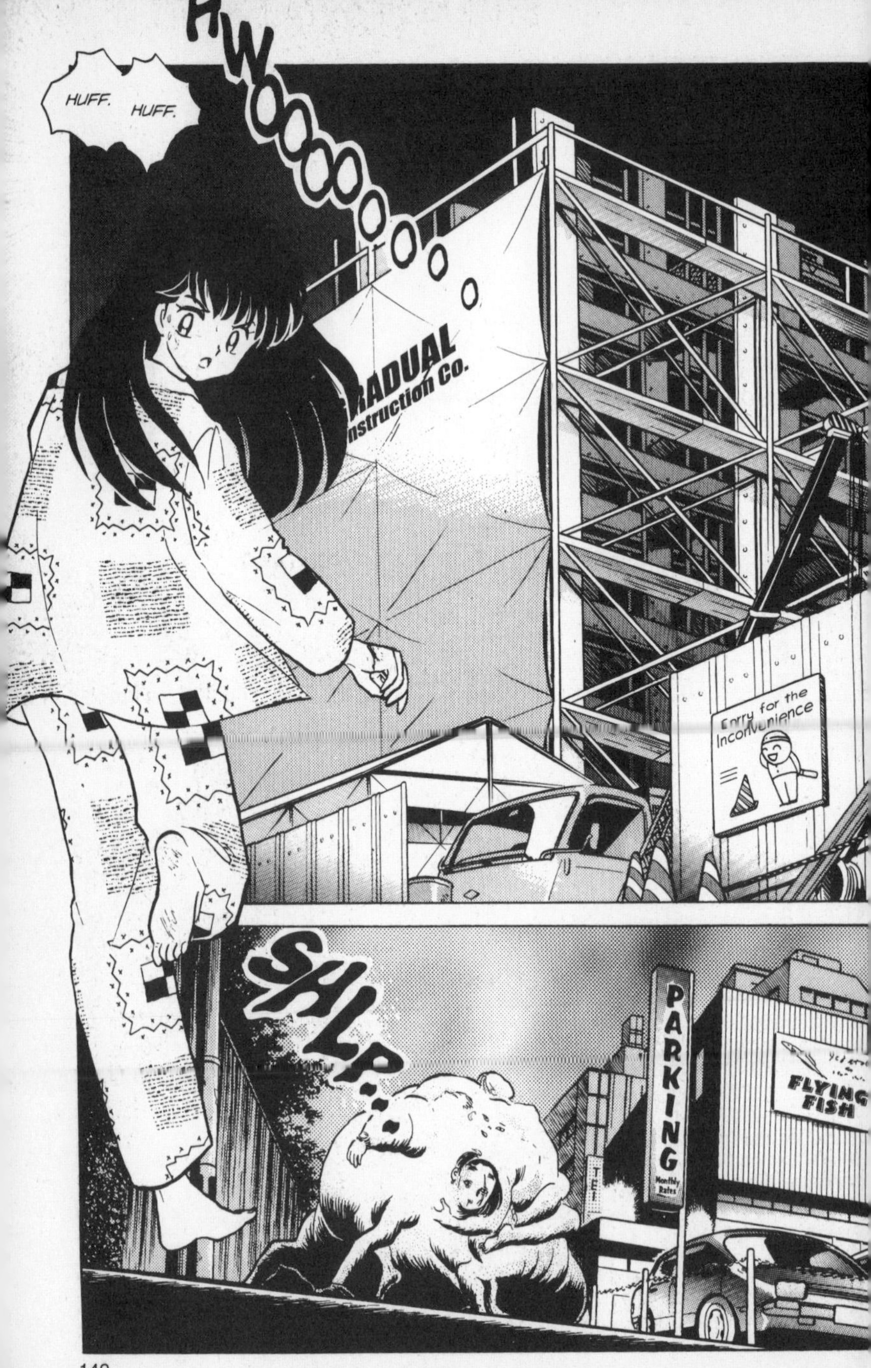
HWOOOOOOO...
HUFF. HUFF.
GRADUAL
Construction Co.
Sorry for the Inconvenience
SHLP...
PARKING
Monthly Rates
TEI
FLYING FISH

THIS THING IS SLOW...
ITS MIND MAY BE IN THAT NOH MASK...

...BUT ITS BODY IS PIECED TOGETHER FROM ITS VICTIMS...
...AND THAT MUST BE HARD TO COORD-INATE.
ZHH...

MAYBE IT WON'T BE ABLE TO FOLLOW ME UP HERE...
DONG

DONG DONG DONG DONG
ZLB...
...

BAAAD GIRRRL...

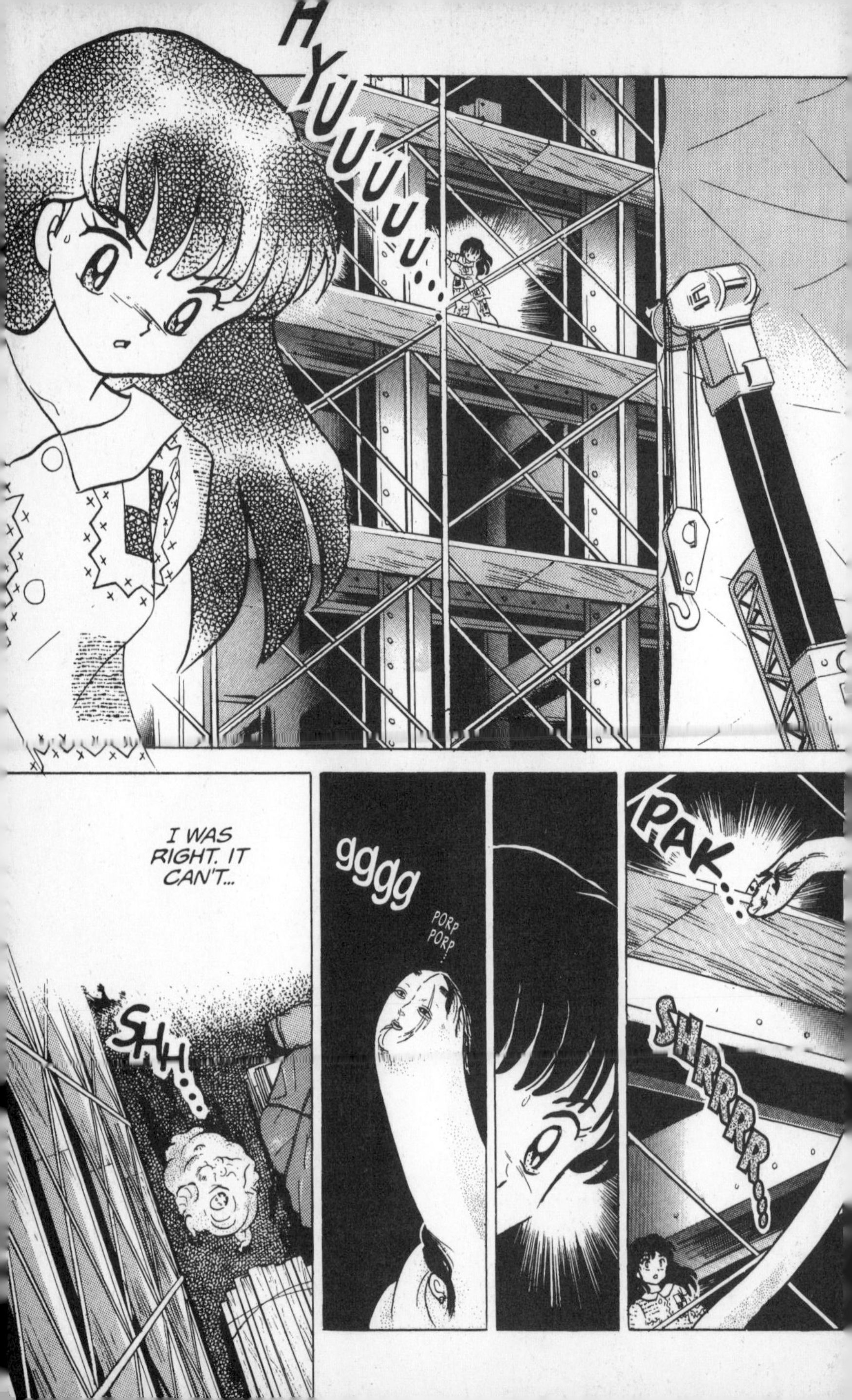
HYUUUUUU...
PAK...
SHRRR...
gggg
PORP PORP
I WAS RIGHT. IT CAN'T...
SHH...

ZHH
ZH
ZH
BOUNG
!
ZZZSHH
PAK
PAK
EEEEYAAA!!

CLAWS OF STEEL !!
SHRED
BLECHA

WELL.
AND I THOUGHT YOU'D BE EATEN BY NOW.
KAGOME!
INU-YASHA...
WAAA! I'M SO HAAAPPY!
OH, SOTA!
TMP
...
INU-YASHA WILL HELP US!
DON'T BE AFRAID NOW.
Y-YEAH.
NOD NOD
HEH.

WELL, I'M NOT SAYING THAT I *WON'T* HELP...
BUT FIRST...

HUH...?

LET'S HEAR AN APOLOGY...
...FOR WHAT YOU DID THE LAST TIME.

WHAT ARE YOU TALKING ABOUT?
DON'T PRETEND YOU'VE FOR-GOTTEN.

JUST... GO!!
BOOT
YOU BOOT ME ASIDE BECAUSE I'M IN YOUR WAY...
...AND THEN EXPECT ME TO HELP YOU?
FEH...
WH... OH.
OH, THAT...
SHE REALLY FORGOT...?!
YOU MEAN...
YOU WERE ACTUALLY BOTHERED BY THAT?
NO!
I JUST FELT LIKE REMINIS-CING!

...
OKAY, OKAY!
I APOLOGIZE.
HOW'S THAT?

...TENSE ABOUT SOMETHING...?
...ALL KINDA...

AM I IMAGINING IT...OR IS INU-YASHA...
B·BMP
B·BMP
B·BMP

DOESN'T IT MEAN... ***ANYTHING*** TO HER...?
RRRH
...

HO HO HO...
plip
plip...
ZZH...

YOU DAAARE...
...TO SPLIT MY PRETTY BODY...?
UGH.
AN UGLY ONE, AREN'T YOU?
WHAT KIND OF DEMON ARE YOU, EH?
ZHH...

INU-YASHA!
ITS MIND IS IN THE NOH MASK...
AND IT HAS A SHARD OF THE SHIKON JEWEL IN ITS FOREHEAD.
OH HO.

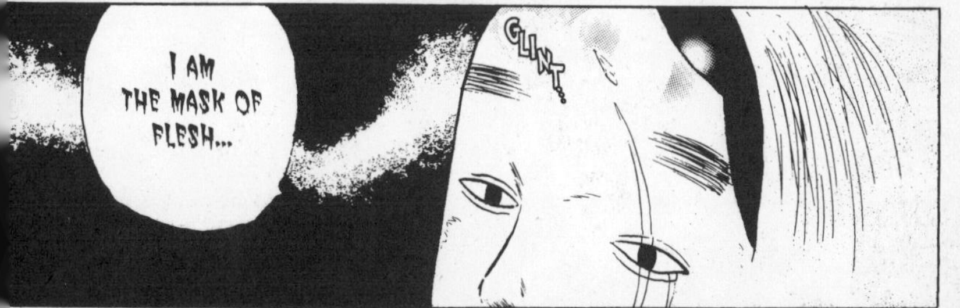
I AM THE MASK OF FLESH...
GLINT...

ALL I WANT IS A BODY...OF MY OWNNN. I KEEP MYSELF ALIIIVE... WITH THE BODIES...OF OTHERS...

...BUT MORTALLL BODIES...

...BREAK SO EEEASILY... YESSS?

TO MAKE THE BODY I WANT...

...I NNNEED MORE SHARDS OF THE JEWEL.

GLINT

HUH.
I'D SAY YOU'VE BEEN DEVOURING TOO MANY MORTALS LATELY...
KRAK
BWA
THEY'VE MADE YOU FAT!!
ALWAYS... ROOM... FOR ONE MORRRE.
GCH GCH
ZZHH

NOT FOR *THIS* ONE !!

SHLUBBB
I'M DISAP-POINTED. IT LOOKED...
HE DID IT...?!
ZHLGG
!
NOW *THAT'S* MORE LIKE IT!
HSSH

WHAT ?!

KRNCH

MORRRTALS... ARE SO GULLLLLIBLLLLE...

GRTCH

GTCH GCH

SCROLL NINE

HALF A DEMON IS WORSE THAN ONE

GRRNN
GRK GK
HYUUUUUUU...
UHH...
GRN GRN
I CAN UUUSE...A GOOD... STRONG... AAARM...
GRN
SHLUP...

WE'VE GOT TO GET THE JEWEL-SHARD OUT OF ITS MASK...
IT'S NO USE ATTACKING THE BODY!

HO HO HO...
GLINT...

POP POP...
TNNG TNNG

YOU ARE MINE NOW. YOU ARE... MEEEE...
ggg...
GWAH

WILL YOU...
...KEEP YOUR SLIMY HANDS *OFF* ME!
WUX WUX
YEAH!
NOTHIN' CAN BEAT INU-YASHA!
TNG

DACH
HYAAAH!
LET'S *END* THIS!
WA
gg
gg
gg

WHEW.
HOW'S THAT?
MNNG..
ZHH...
HSHH
BAAAD BOYYY...
SHLUP
KRAK
YAAAAY!

THE OTHER HALF OF THE MASK HAS THE SHARD...
WE HAVE TO GET IT OUT BEFORE IT CAN...
INU-YASHA, DON'T LET YOUR GUARD DOWN!

HSSSH

gggg...
!

OH...

WHAT ?!

I-INU...
YASHA...

GHNG...

HYUUUUUUU...

NO...

FSH

KAGOME!

LET GO OF THE MASK!

WHAT...?!

DON'T MOVE AN INCH!
THE TETSU-SAIGA!!

SHK
PINNG...
WOOOSH
WE DID IT...
HEH...
SHHP...
INU-YASHA...

KAGOME--
ARE YOU ALL RIGHT ?!

...
GOOD. I'M GLAD.
SHKK

THANKS...
Y-YEAH... I'M FINE...

NOW SHE REALLY OWES ME.
HEH.

...ALMOST LIKE HE REALLY CARES...
HE'S ACTING...

...
LET'S JUST *SEE* HER TRY TO DO ANYTHING ON HER OWN FROM NOW ON.

THE MASK...

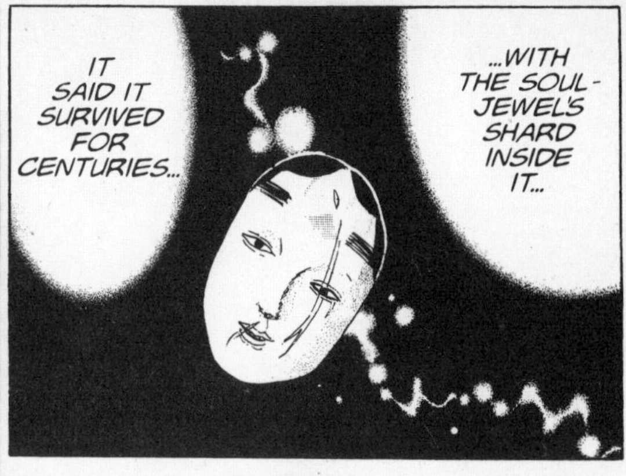
IT SAID IT SURVIVED FOR CENTURIES...
...WITH THE SOUL-JEWEL'S SHARD INSIDE IT...

WHICH MEANS...
...OTHER SHARDS COULD HAVE SURVIVED TO THE PRESENT, TOO...

twee...
WHAT... ?
MORNING... ?

gasp
AAAA !!
MY MATH EXAM !!

VROOM
BYE!
INU-YASHA, YOU GO BACK IN TIME, I'LL COME LATER!

UM...
...I THOUGHT YOU WERE REALLY AWESOME...
...THANKS...

SSSHHHH

EH?

...BUT I'M OVER THE HUMP NOW!
I'M HALF-DEAD...
SCRIBBLE SCRIBBLE SCRIBBLE
I CAN DO IT!

DONE!
DONE!
DONE!
IF I DON'T HURRY, INU-YASHA'S GONNA GET ALL TESTY AGAIN. WHAT'S HIS PROBLEM?
'COURSE THIS TIME...
...HE REALLY WAS KINDA...
...HEROIC.

SKRiiK
MAKING YOUR BOY-FRIEND WAIT, HUH?
GOOD LUCK, KAGOME!

HE IS *NOT* MY BOY-FRIEND!
WILL YOU *STOP* THAT?!

WE WERE JUST THROWN TOGETHER BY A CRUEL TWIST OF FATE!
HUH?

I HOPE SHE MAKES IT...
SHE'LL LOVE THESE THERA-PEUTIC HERBS..
AS FOR THE UNFOR-TUNATE HOJO.
Matinee
¥1000
AND I THOUGHT SHE LIKED HOJO...
IT WAS GONNA BE THEIR FIRST DATE, TOO...
'SFUNNY...

OKAY, SOTA...
I'M OFF AGAIN.
HWFF!!...
BUT... DON'CHA THINK YOUR PACK'S TOO FULL?
A GIRL HAS A LOT OF NEEDS, YOU KNOW.
TOOM...
FOOM
GOMP
EEEP?!
BAH.
CRETIN.
WHAT THE HELL ARE YOU DOING?!

HEY...

HWA

LET'S GO!

HE'S CARRYIN' YOUR PACK...

THAT'S NICE, HUH?

OH, *SURE*.

BUT...

HE *WAS* WAITING FOR ME... WASN'T HE?

WHILE ACROSS TOWN...

SIGH

GOSH...

SHE MUST BE ILL AGAIN...

...THE LIMITS OF NAIVETÉ ARE BEING TESTED.

SCROLL TEN
FOXFIRE

THIS... THIS FOOD...
KAGOME, IT'S...
...IT'S GOOD!
CUP 'O
SUPER NOODLES
MISO SOUP RAMEN 0.5

REALLY...
I'M SO HAPPY FOR YOU...

DON'T YOU WANT ANY?
HOW CAN YOU IN A PLACE LIKE THIS?
CAW CAW CAW CAW
HYUUUUUUUU
SHLRRP

IS THAT... FOXFIRE... ?

YOU... HOLD SHARDS... OF THE JEWEL OF SOULS...

WHAT ?!

A DEMON...

PONNG
GIVE... THEM !

I'LL KILL YOU...!
KOMP
SKRTCH SKRTCH
HSSH

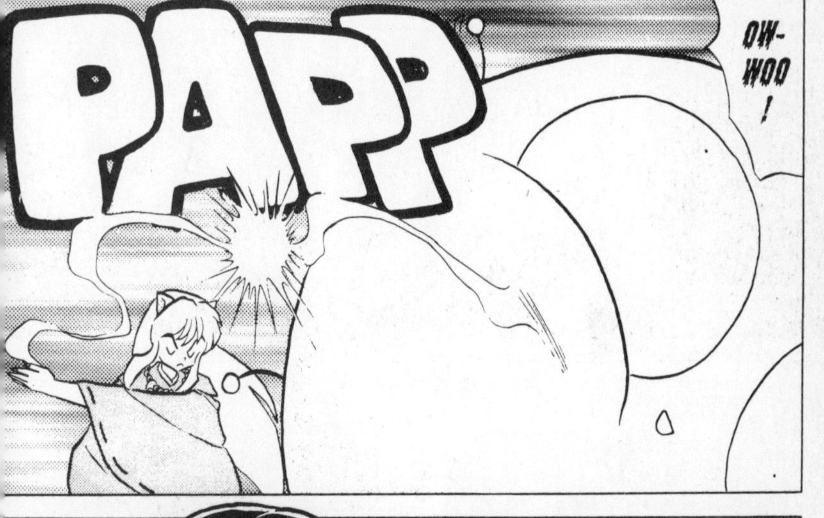

POP
YOWWW
THROB
EH?
A KID...

HE'S SO CUUUUUUTE...
gasp

WHAT DO YOU THINK THIS IS?
tee hee
CAN I HUG HIM NEXT ?

EH ?!
ZUMP

HUH ?

AAAA!! MY STUFF!!
VP VP VP VP VP VP

SHARDS OF THE JEWEL !
AT LAST !

HWORRRR
WAHAHAHA! THANKS... AND FAREWELL!
YOU...
CHING...
HE'S GONE!
SHHK SHHK
GYNN
KLAK KLAK
SHHK SHHK
WHY ARE YOU AFTER THE SHIKON JEWEL?
MOOP...
MINE IS A TRAGIC TAIL.

YOUR FATHER WAS KILLED... ?
AVENGE...?

MY NAME IS SHIPPŌ... AND I'M TRYING TO AVENGE MY PA!

OH-HO. THEN YOU WERE HOPING...
fsh fsh

THOSE ARE MINE BY RIGHT!
WHAT'RE *YOU* DOING WITH THOSE ?!
HEY !
BWA

I DON'T NEED *ANYTHING* TO INCREASE MY POWERS. UNDERSTAND ?
I ONLY...

...THAT THE JEWEL-SHARDS WOULD INCREASE YOUR POWERS ENOUGH TO AVENGE HIM, EH?

HUH ?!
ARE YOU LIS- TENING TO ME?!

HWUUUUU...
RAAAAAAAAAAH
RURURUM...
BOOOOOOM
EH?!
SOME-THING COMES...

RRRROOOOO
LET THE *HUNT* BEGIN, MANTEN!
AND LET IT RUN LONG, HITEN.

GW
GW
GW

WHAT...
NIHIHIHI
D... DEMONS... ?!

HYEEE HEE- HEE- HEE!
A-HA HAHA HAHA HA!
HYNNG
CLAP CLAP
MMM...?
SNORT

HWA
PXXT PXXT

VMP
SHHH

OH, GREAT PLEASURE, HITEN.
HSSSSSHH
AH, WHAT PLEASURE, EH, MANTEN?
GLMP
AND STILL AM I FLOODED WITH POWER UNTAPPED. THESE SHARDS OF THE SHIKON JEWEL ARE WONDROUS, INDEED.

THOSE THINGS...
THEY'RE SLAUGHTERING EVERY DEMON WHO HAS ONE!
BUT WHO ARE THEY?
RATATATA
THE THUNDER BROTHERS...
"THUNDER"?
DO YOU MEAN HITEN AND MANTEN?
I'D HEARD THEY WERE A RIGHT COUPLE O' RUFFIANS, BUT...
WHO CARES WHAT THEY ARE?
DEFEAT THEM...AND WE'VE GOT A WHOLE LOT OF SHIKON SHARDS IN OUR HANDS ALL AT ONCE.

DON'T MAKE ME LAUGH.
YOU DON'T HAVE A CHANCE AGAINST THEM.
EH?

YOU'RE HALF-DEMON, AREN'T YOU?
I CAN SMELL THE HUMAN IN YOU.

MY FATHER WAS A *REAL* DEMON!
IF HE COULDN'T HANDLE THEM, WHAT CAN A MUTT LIKE YOU--

SHIPPŌ! WHAT KIND OF THING IS THAT TO...

BONK

HSSSH

WAAAA!
BONK BONK BONK
NOW, NOW, M'LORD, IS THAT ANY WAY FOR A DEMON TO BEHAVE?
STOP IT!!

I'M SORRY, I'M SO SORRY!
JUST REMEM-BER THIS.
BOW BOW

AS A GESTURE OF APOLOGY...
SHFF SHFF

ZNG

PLAP

WAHAHAHAHA! UNLESS YOU REMOVE THAT SPELL-SCROLL, THAT STATUE OF JIZŌ STAYS RIGHT THERE!
ZNNNN
YOU SON OF A...

I HATE TO GET ROUGH WITH A VIXEN, BUT...

...I NEED YOU TO SLEEP FOR A WHILE!
DNK

HEY, THAT HURT!
EEP.

FOX-FIRE!!
GWM

I'M STARTING TO GET MAD!
VSH
GIVE THOSE BACK!
I'LL LURE THOSE MURDERERS OUT WITH THESE!
SHA
THE SHIKON JEWEL SHARDS...
OH!
KAGOME!
CHASE HIM AFTER YOU TAKE OFF THIS SCROLL!
KAGOME, THE SCROLL!
hss...
THEN SURELY I SHOULD STIR EVEN MORE FEMALE HEARTS THAN MY ELDER BROTHER...
...BUT A FEW MORE HAIRS THAN THESE THREE.
pt pt
WOULD THAT I HAD...
ALAS.

HMM... ?

HWA...

WHY DON'T YOU *COME*, YOU...

SHF...

gulp

OH...
AH, YOU ADMIRE MY WRAP...
ASK YOUR FATHER FOR ONE. I BELIEVE HE HAD ONE...JUST LIKE IT.
PAT PAT
P-PAPA...
YOU KILLED HIM...
AND YOU'LL *DIE*.
SHAA
WAK

TOOM
FOR IF YOU DO NOT...
BRING IT OUT...
YOU HAVE A SHARD OF THE JEWEL, LITTLE PUP...
UGH...
N... NO...! NO!
EH?!
SHP
OH...
I... I HIT HIM...!

TO BE CONTINUED...

EDITOR'S RECOMMENDATIONS

Did you like INUYASHA? Here's what we recommend you try next:

RANMA 1/2 is the manga Rumiko Takahashi was working on previous to *INUYASHA*. It's more comedic than *INUYASHA*—sort of a cross between a screwball comedy and a martial-arts action movie—but it's chock full of unique characters and complicated romantic entanglements.

© 1988 Rumiko Takahashi/Shogakukan

MAISON IKKOKU is Takahashi's most romantic series. It's set in modern-day Japan, and traces the lives of the residents of a boarding house. It's intense, it's angsty, and it's one of the most absorbing manga romances ever written.

© 1984 Rumiko Takahashi/Shogakukan

CERES: CELESTIAL LEGEND is a sort of supernatural mystery by *FUSHIGI YÛGI*'s creator, Yû Watase. It's about a modern-day 16-year-old girl whose body houses a legendary power, and her family is determined to kill her in order to suppress it. The story draws heavily on Japanese legends.

© 1997 Yuu Watase/Shogakukan

A TEST OF SKILLS... A BATTLE OF WILLS!

犬夜叉

INUYASHA Anime DVD and Man[illegible] – Now Available

Tag team players can switch between characters seamlessly!

Engage in 2 player and single player combat or tag team battles!

Launch double attacks with a team member!

From the hot new Television Show on Cartoon Network!

Based on the comic by the great manga artist, Rumiko Takahashi, Bandai is proud to present INUYASHA for the PlayStation game console! Battle your way through the thrilling world of INUYASHA and unlock new characters for hours of pulse-pounding fighting action! Go head-to-head against a friend, or team up in tag-team and versus modes! In this fight for fun, you'll always come out the winner!

INUYASHA
A Feudal Fairy Tale

SPRINGDALE PUBLIC LIBRARY
405 S. Pleasant
Springdale, AR 72764

[illegible] Inuyasha logo, and all related characters and elements are trademarks of Shogakukan Production Co., Ltd. © 2003 Rumiko Takahaski/Shogakukan-YTV-Sunrise. © 2002-2003 BANDAI. This product is manufactured, distributed and sold under license from ShoPro Entertainment. All Rights Reserved. PlayStation and the PlayStation logos are registered trademarks of Sony Computer Entertainment Inc.

COMPLETE OUR SURVEY AND LET US KNOW WHAT YOU THINK!

☐ Please check here if you DO NOT wish to receive information or future offers from VIZ

Name: ______________________

Address: ______________________

City: ______________ **State:** ________ **Zip:** ____________

E-mail: ______________________

☐ **Male** ☐ **Female** **Date of Birth (mm/dd/yyyy):** ____/____/______ (**Under 13? Parental consent required**)

What race/ethnicity do you consider yourself? (please check one)

☐ Asian/Pacific Islander ☐ Black/African American ☐ Hispanic/Latino

☐ Native American/Alaskan Native ☐ White/Caucasian ☐ Other: ____________

What VIZ product did you purchase? (check all that apply and indicate title purchased)

☐ DVD/VHS ______________________

☐ Graphic Novel ______________________

☐ Magazines ______________________

☐ Merchandise ______________________

Reason for purchase: (check all that apply)

☐ Special offer ☐ Favorite title ☐ Gift

☐ Recommendation ☐ Other ______________________

Where did you make your purchase? (please check one)

☐ Comic store ☐ Bookstore ☐ Mass/Grocery Store

☐ Newsstand ☐ Video/Video Game Store ☐ Other: ____________

☐ Online (site: ______________________)

What other VIZ properties have you purchased/own? ______________________

____

How many anime and/or manga titles have you purchased in the last year? How many were VIZ titles? **(please check one from each column)**

ANIME	MANGA	VIZ
☐ None	☐ None	☐ None
☐ 1-4	☐ 1-4	☐ 1-4
☐ 5-10	☐ 5-10	☐ 5-10
☐ 11+	☐ 11+	☐ 11+

I find the pricing of VIZ products to be: **(please check one)**

☐ Cheap ☐ Reasonable ☐ Expensive

What genre of manga and anime would you like to see from VIZ? **(please check two)**

☐ Adventure ☐ Comic Strip ☐ Detective ☐ Fighting

☐ Horror ☐ Romance ☐ Sci-Fi/Fantasy ☐ Sports

What do you think of VIZ's new look?

☐ Love It ☐ It's OK ☐ Hate It ☐ Didn't Notice ☐ No Opinion

THANK YOU! Please send the completed form to:

NJW Research
42 Catharine St.
Poughkeepsie, NY 12601

All information provided will be used for internal purposes only. We promise not to sell or otherwise divulge your information.

NO PURCHASE NECESSARY. Requests not in compliance with all terms of this form will not be acknowledged or returned. All submissions are subject to verification and become the property of VIZ, LLC. Fraudulent submission, including use of multiple addresses or P.O. boxes to obtain additional VIZ information or offers may result in prosecution. VIZ reserves the right to withdraw or modify any terms of this form. Void where prohibited, taxed, or restricted by law. VIZ will not be liable for lost, misdirected, mutilated, illegible, incomplete or postage-due mail. © 2003 VIZ, LLC. All Rights Reserved. VIZ, LLC, property titles, characters, names and plots therein under license to VIZ, LLC. All Rights Reserved.